King

Queen

Pharaoh

Clown

cowboy

flamenco Dancer

Bride

Santa

opera Singer

Sheriff

Artist

Witch

Ice Skater

Superhero

Cave Woman   Cave Man

Fairy

Baker

Magician　　　Knight

Fireman

Sheikh

Astronaut

BMX

Rock'n'Roll Dancer

Baby

Rock'n'Roll Dancer

Baby

Hippy   Lumberjack

Emperor

Indian Dancer

Painter   farmer

Skip

Muscian

Surgeon   Chinese Lady

Dwarf

Tarzan

Skier

Scientist   Butcher

Pirate

Mountaineer

Surfer

Vicar

High Jumper

Weightlifter

Juggler

conductor

Basketball Player

Waiter

Football Player